Life in the BOREAL FOREST

BRENDA Z. GUIBERSON

paintings by **GENNADY SPIRIN**

Groundwood Books   House of Anansi Press
Toronto

For Bill

—B. Z. G.

For all lovers of nature

—G. S.

The author would also like to thank the following individuals
for their help in vetting the manuscript:

JIM STEWART, research scientist, Natural Resources Canada
SAMANTHA SONG, boreal ecologist, Environment Canada
WENDY CALVERT, wildlife biologist, Environment Canada
ERIC ALLEN, research scientist, Canadian Forest Service

Thanks to Laura Godwin, Noa Wheeler, Patrick Collins,
and all those at Holt who helped with this book

Text copyright © 2009 by Brenda Z. Guiberson
Illustrations copyright © 2009 by Gennady Spirin
Map on page 32 by Brenda Z. Guiberson
Reprinted by arrangement with Henry Holt and Company, LLC.

Groundwood Books / House of Anansi Press
110 Spadina Avenue, Suite 801, Toronto, Ontario M5V 2K4

We acknowledge for their financial support of our publishing program the Book Publishing Industry Development Program (BPIDP).

Library and Archives Canada Cataloguing in Publication
Guiberson, Brenda Z
Life in the boreal forest / Brenda Z. Guiberson ; paintings by
Gennady Spirin.
ISBN 978-0-88899-956-6
1. Taiga ecology–Juvenile literature. 2. Taigas–Juvenile
literature. I. Spirin, Gennadii II. Title.
QH541.5.T3G83 2009   j578.73'7   C2008-907660-5

This book is printed on Yalan matte-coated paper, which contains 50% post-consumer recycled fibers and is acid-free.
It is processed chlorine-free and is manufactured using biogas energy.
Designed by Patrick Collins
Printed and bound in China

Life in the Boreal Forest

Many organizations, schools, and government agencies are involved in preserving the boreal forest and the creatures who live there. To find out what some of these concerned groups of people are doing and recommending, you can visit the Web sites listed below.

Alberta Wilderness Association	www.albertawilderness.ca
Animals of the Boreal Forest	www.cdli.ca/CITE/boreal_forest_animals.htm
Boreal Songbird Initiative	www.borealbirds.org
Canadian Boreal Initiative	www.borealcanada.ca
Cornell Lab of Ornithology	www.birds.cornell.edu/AllAboutBirds/BirdGuide
Endangered Species Links	http://eelink.net/EndSpp
Environment Canada	www.ec.gc.ca
International Boreal Conservation Campaign	www.pewtrusts.org
Maine Audubon	www.maineaudubon.org
National Audubon Society	www.audubon.org
Natural Resources Defense Council	www.nrdc.org
Nature Conservancy	www.nature.org
Northern Alaska Environmental Center	www.northern.org
Ontario Nature	www.ontarionature.org/enviroandcons/boreal/index.html
Save Our Boreal Birds	www.saveourborealbirds.org
Sierra Club	www.sierraclub.org/ecoregions/boreal.asp
Taiga or Boreal Forest	www.marietta.edu/~biol/biomes/boreal.htm
U.S. Fish and Wildlife Service	www.fws.gov
Whooping Crane Conservation Association	www.whoopingcrane.com
Woods Hole Research Center	www.whrc.org/borealnamerica/index.htm
World Wildlife Fund–Canada	www.wwf.ca

Tika tika tika swee swee! A Tennessee warbler sings in a forest so huge that it covers one-third of the earth's total forest area. It grows across Alaska, Canada, Scandinavia, and Russia. A swath of trees this big has many names, like taiga and boreal forest. Boreal means northern, from Boreas, the Greek god of the north wind.

A forest this far north is buried in ice and snow during winter. But the summertime lakes teem with fish, and bogs swarm with insects. Many hungry creatures need this forest to survive.

From points south, including our own backyards, birds fly to this northern forest by the thousands, millions, until there are billions. They arrive when the snow melts and work fast to raise chicks before winter's return.

Snap, snap! The Tennessee warbler snatches up budworms for her brood. *Plish, ploosh!* A loon dives for minnows and leeches. *Burble, gurgle!* White pelicans fish for some of the sixty-eight kilograms of food needed to raise each chick.

Ker lee loo! Even the whooping cranes come, the last few hundred birds fighting extinction as they flap on great wings toward their only nesting place in the wild.

While visiting birds try to double their weight before the fall migration, the year-round forest residents prepare for snow survival.

Chawchaw! The beavers bite into wood. *Crackle! Thwak!* Trees tumble. Beavers haul branches underwater to eat when thick ice traps them for months in their frozen lodge and pond.

*H*up, *hup!* A snowshoe hare, molting her brown summer coat into thick winter white, is desperate for a meal. After a ten-year cycle of a growing population, the forest had far too many hares and not enough food for them to eat. Most of the hares died, most of the low-growing food is gone, and stressed plants are making toxins to keep twig eaters away. The snowshoe hare is starving.

But the moose is not. He reaches high to browse on small trees regrowing after a fire. *Slurp! Crack!* When he breaks a branch, the hare will have something extra to eat. *Nibble, nibble.*

Grrowll! The bear needs a thirteen-centimeter layer of body fat to survive a long winter sleep. In one frenzied day he gobbles seventy thousand berries. His droppings spread seeds that grow into new bushes.

The lynx is hungry for snowshoe hare. The cat huddles quietly, waiting for one to pass. Last year there were thousands of hares. This year there are only a few. It is a bleak time for hare hunters.

But the spruce trees have produced a splendid crop of cones. Crossbills flock in. With their crisscrossed beaks, they pry out three thousand seeds a day. They store extra seeds in a throat pouch. Dropped seeds may grow into new spruce trees as long as there is no human development to stop the cycle.

Aoohooooo! Hungry wolves howl. As the temperature plunges, billions of singing and honking birds migrate south to our lakes and yards. But the forest is not quiet. *Clink, clunk!* In the frozen days before snow, ice cracks and shatters with every step. The noisy lynx cannot prowl.

Tiny voles shiver and shake as they wait for snow to fall. *Trrrrrr!* Many do not survive.

But trillions of evergreen trees, each with millions of needles, continue to make their own food. A fungus growing in their roots helps them absorb water. The needles combine the water with carbon dioxide from the air, sunlight, and a green chemical called chlorophyll. The process makes a sugary feast for both trees and fungi. It also adds oxygen to the air. Throughout the boreal forest, trees cleanse the air for all to breathe.

Hush-a-shush. Snow falls to warm the forest. So much snow, so beautiful and varied that the Inuit people have given some kinds a special name.

Annui, falling snow, covers the forest like a soft blanket. *Qali* is snow caught in the arms of trees. Here the squirrel snuggles in for a cozy nap. *Api* is snow piled on the ground. *Rrap! Rrap!* A raven rolls in it to take a bath. As the snow piles higher, the hare can reach new food.

When the snow is fifteen centimeters deep, voles dig their tunnels. *Scritch, scratch.* In warm winter homes, they munch on buried plants and raise their babies.

The bear snoozes under a fallen tree, but his sleep is restless. *Chip, chop!* Now that the soggy ground is frozen, a logging crew is cutting trees. Each year brings new loggers, miners, and peat harvesters. The boreal forest is disappearing fast.

The moose has shed his antlers and with his long legs can step through deep snow to search for food. But the little red fox struggles.

Pitpatpat, the hare packs down easy trails with her huge snowshoe feet.

Now the fox can jitter-jog down the hare highway. *Scritch, scritch!* In the dark days of winter, ears are always alert, and the fox hears voles in the snow tunnels. He dives for a meal. The great horned owl hears them too. *Swoosh!* Another vole gets snagged with long, sharp talons.

The temperature drops even further to minus forty degrees Celsius and stays there for two weeks. The lynx tries to sniff out dinner, but the air is too cold to carry a scent.

Whoom, whoosh! A sledder on a toboggan urges his dogs across the frozen beaver pond.

Chip, crunch! Inside their lodge, the beavers munch on stored leaves and bark. Under insulating layers of snow, logs, and frozen mud, their winter home is twenty-seven degrees warmer than the outside air. They sip the only unfrozen water in the forest. Now and then, they swim under the thick ice to gather up a new refrigerated meal.

With everything frozen, the forest has a water shortage. But the coniferous trees have thin, needlelike leaves with a thick, waxy layer to hold in moisture. The sleeping bear does not need to drink all winter.

The lynx gets her water from gulps of snow. A trapper spots her supersize pawprints and would like to have her thick winter coat. He sets a trap.

With so few hares this year, the lynx prowls far away, through a crisscross of icy roads and oil pipelines, desperate to find a meal. Finally she hooks an ermine, but it is only one-fifth the size of a hare.

After months of darkness, the sun moves up in the sky and the snow softens. But the frigid night freezes it into icy crust. The fox can't break through to the voles, the moose scrapes his legs on sharp edges, and a ptarmigan sleeping in a snow-drift gets trapped inside.

Finally snow falls again. *Hush-a-shush*. Hungry caribou use the snow piles to reach food on high branches. All winter, they depend on lichen that needs clean air and hundred-year-old trees to grow.

But every year, with more human development, fewer old trees remain.

As the days get longer, the thaw begins. *Drip-dribble-drip.* Snow and ice melt. But some of the ground, called permafrost, has been frozen for thousands of years and is still frozen. Water can't drain through the icy dirt so it seeps into soggy bogs. Sphagnum moss sops it up like a sponge until it holds about twenty times its weight in water and prevents flooding.

In this chilly, squishy soil, there are swarms of mosquitoes and flies but not much food for plants. So the pitcher plant makes sweet nectar that attracts a fly. Trapped by stiff hairs, the fly slips into the pool at the bottom and joins a pile of ants, grasshoppers, mosquitoes, and a frog that are being slowly digested by this carnivorous plant.

*S*quish, *squash!* The moose dips under the beaver pond for a mouthful of greens. He needs to eat twenty-three kilograms of plants each day to replace lost fat and grow new antlers.

The beavers are already chopping down trees. When a birch bounces onto the spongy ground, the near-starved snowshoe hare hops up for a nibble.

A fir tree is sending out a warning. Budworms! The tree makes a foul-tasting toxin to slow down their eating. Other trees get a whiff and quickly make their own chemical defense.

Tennessee warblers fly in. After a long migration from a Mexican rain forest, they are famished. *Snap, snap!* Warblers gobble budworms and help the trees with pest control.

For this year, the snowshoe hare raises just two leverets. With so few hares to provide food, the lynx will not raise a kitten. Instead she wanders farther than ever before, close to new human settlements and over new roads, in search of food.

Everywhere she hears *chirp, cheep, tweet, honk*. The billions of birds, more than two hundred species, have returned. They seek the trees and lakes, budworms and leeches, and everything needed to raise their chicks. It is a new season of life in the boreal forest.

🌿 *Author's Note* 🌿

The boreal forest takes up 35 percent of Canada's total land mass and 77 percent of our total forest lands. This forest is one of the world's best places to store carbon, thus providing a crucial protection against global warming.

Yet today the boreal forest is in danger. The extraction of oil from thousands of acres of northern lands is one of the most destructive human activities for this forest. Vast areas are also under siege from clear-cut logging, mining, moss harvesting, dam building, and other development. Much more activity is scheduled far into the future. And global warming is already causing severe damage from new insect infestation.

Today the boreal forest is as big and important as the tropical rain forests. It is so vast that when maximum growth occurs in spring and summer, the worldwide levels of carbon dioxide fall and levels of oxygen rise. This forest—which surrounds and protects countless bogs, marshes, lakes, and rivers—encompasses the largest freshwater system in the world. It cleans the air, filters water, prevents flooding, provides for people and wildlife, and regulates global climate. It has been providing these services for thousands of years, for free! And yet few people know about the boreal forest or understand how vital it is to us and to the earth.

Boreal creatures can digest twigs and live under the snow, but they struggle with the drastic changes made by humans. The woodland caribou, wood bison, whooping crane, wolf, wolverine, lynx, bear, bull trout, cougar, marten, and harlequin duck are among the boreal creatures endangered or threatened today. And many, many species of songbirds will disappear if their nesting grounds in the boreal forest disappear.

Our own survival and that of most of the world's species are at stake. Today, more than 95 percent of the world's old-growth forests are gone. Tropical rain forests are disappearing fast. What can we do? We can stop wasting paper. And for the planet's sake we must drastically cut our consumption of fossil fuels. It is essential to protect this forest now so that it will be there for the future. This will only happen if we can find a way to work together and succeed in convincing our governments that they need to act with us to stop global warming. Canadians have a vast forest treasure in our backyard and limited opportunity to save it. All of us must act quickly before it is too late. If we succeed, we help life in the boreal forest, ourselves, and all of the earth as well.

BOREAL FOREST (TAIGA)